WONDER
BUGS

Consultants: David W. Inouye, Brian D. Inouye
Illustrators: Robert Cremins, Stuart Armstrong

Copyright © 2000 by the National Geographic Society

Published by
The National Geographic Society
John M. Fahey, Jr., President and Chief Executive Officer
Gilbert M. Grosvenor, Chairman of the Board
Nina D. Hoffman, Senior Vice President
William R. Gray, Vice President and Director, Book Division

Staff for this Book
Barbara Brownell, Director of Continuities
Marianne R. Koszorus, Senior Art Director
Toni Eugene, Editor
Alexandra Littlehales, Art Director
Marfé Ferguson Delano, Writer-Researcher
Susan V. Kelly, Illustrations Editor
Sharon Kocsis Berry, Illustrations Assistant
Mark A. Caraluzzi, Director of Direct Response Marketing
Heidi Vincent, Product Manager
Vincent P. Ryan, Manufacturing Manager
Lewis R. Bassford, Production Project Manager

Visit our Web site at www.nationalgeographic.com

Library of Congress Catalog Card Number: 132923
ISBN: 0-7922-3459-6

Color separations by Quad Graphics, Martinsburg, West Virginia
Printed in Mexico by R.R. Donnelley & Sons Company

MY FIRST POCKET GUIDE

WONDER BUGS

Marfé Ferguson Delano

Photographs supplied by Animals Animals/Earth Scenes

NATIONAL GEOGRAPHIC SOCIETY

INTRODUCTION

What do insects, which have a body with three segments and six legs, have in common with spiders, which have a body with two segments and eight legs? Both types of creatures have a skeleton on the outside of the body—and both are commonly called bugs.

These pages will introduce you to 35 fascinating bugs. You will meet the biggest, the brightest, and the loudest in the world and learn about other bugs that stand out because of their shape, speed, smell, sting, or survival techniques. Some of the bugs featured are known as true bugs, which are insects with sucking mouthparts.

The bugs in this book come from all over the globe. Many of them may live

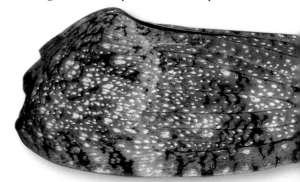

near you. Several of them are found only
in tropical areas.

HOW TO USE THIS BOOK

Insects appear first, followed by spiders.
The insects are organized according to
type. Beetles, which are insects with hard
front wings, are grouped together, true
bugs are together, and so on.

Within each type, the creatures are
arranged by size, from the biggest to the
smallest bug.

Each spread in this book helps you
identify one kind of insect or spider, and
tells you about its size, color, and behavior.
A shaded map shows where in the world
to find each bug. The "Field Notes" entry
gives an interesting fact about the bug.
If you see a word you do not know, look
it up in the Glossary on page 76.

HERCULES BEETLE

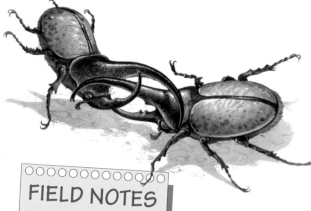

The Hercules beetle is the longest beetle in the world—almost as long as a pencil! Like the hero Hercules in Greek legends, this beetle is amazingly strong. It can lift many times its own weight.

FIELD NOTES

In a fight over a female, Hercules males use their horns to lift their rivals, then slam them down.

A Hercules beetle's fierce-looking horns give this bug its other name, the rhinoceros beetle.

WHERE TO FIND:

SOUTH AMERICA

The Hercules beetle lives among the trees in tropical rain forests of Central and South America.

WHAT TO LOOK FOR:

❋ SIZE
The Hercules beetle can be seven inches long.

❋ COLOR
It has a black or brownish body with black horns.

❋ BEHAVIOR
When a male beetle meets another male, it rubs its wing covers together to make a loud threatening noise.

❋ MORE
The adult beetle feeds on fruit.

GOLIATH BEETLE

 The heaviest insect of all is the Goliath beetle, named after the giant in the Bible story. This big bug can weigh up to four ounces. That is as much as a good-size apple or a quarter-pound hamburger!

WHERE TO FIND:
This enormous beetle can be found in the tropical forests of western and southern Africa.

WHAT TO LOOK FOR:

✳ SIZE
Goliath beetles can be four inches long.

✳ COLOR
Most Goliath beetles are black and white or brown and white.

✳ BEHAVIOR
Goliath beetles fly into treetops to feed on sap. At night they hide under leaves and in hollow logs.

✳ MORE
Some people roast the larvae, or young, of these beetles and eat them.

FIELD NOTES

Despite their size, Goliath beetles are harmless. Some children in Africa keep them as pets.

The body of the Goliath beetle is about the size of a grown-up person's fist.

9

LONGHORN HARLEQUIN BEETLE

 Despite its name, this beautiful beetle has no horns, long or short. It does, however, have incredibly long antennae, which may once have been mistaken for horns.

WHERE TO FIND:
The longhorn harlequin beetle dwells in the rain forests of Central and South America.

WHAT TO LOOK FOR:

✳ **SIZE**
The body of the longhorn harlequin beetle is about three inches long.

✳ **COLOR**
It is covered with a black and yellowish orange pattern, similar to that worn by colorful clowns known as harlequins.

✳ **BEHAVIOR**
These beetles lay their eggs on the trunks of dead fig trees.

✳ **MORE**
They are active both day and night.

Tiny scorpion-like bugs in search of food and mates hitch flights on the back of these beetles.

This beetle uses its extra-long antennae to check out the world around it.

11

TIGER BEETLE

Tiger beetles are not only ferocious predators but also take the prize for the fastest running insect. Some kinds can run two feet a second. That's the equivalent of a racehorse running 250 miles an hour!

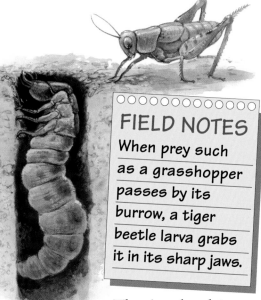

FIELD NOTES

When prey such as a grasshopper passes by its burrow, a tiger beetle larva grabs it in its sharp jaws.

The tiger beetle's large eyes give it sharp vision—the better to hunt with.

WHERE TO FIND:
Tiger beetles can be found throughout much of the world. They often inhabit sandy areas.

WHAT TO LOOK FOR:

✴ SIZE
Tiger beetles range in size from less than 1/2 inch to about 2 1/2 inches.

✴ COLOR
They can be a shiny bronze, blue, green, purple, or orange.

✴ BEHAVIOR
Tiger beetles can fly but prefer to run.

✴ MORE
Tiger beetles eat other insects. The beetles chase their prey down and seize it in their strong jaws.

13

LANTERN CLICK BEETLE

 The brightest bug of all is this click beetle. Its greenish yellow glow outshines the light of all other light-producing insects. These beetles use the light to attract mates.

WHERE TO FIND:
Also called the headlight beetle, this insect lives in the West Indies and Central and South America.

NORTH AMERICA

SOUTH AMERICA

WHAT TO LOOK FOR:

✳ SIZE
This beetle is about one inch long.

✳ COLOR
It can be dark brown or black.

✳ BEHAVIOR
Like all click beetles, the lantern beetle makes a sharp clicking sound when it flips from its back onto its feet.

✳ MORE
The larva of this beetle also glows. It preys on the larvae of other beetles.

The lantern click beetle's light is produced by two organs on its thorax, the middle section of its body.

BOMBARDIER BEETLE

 This little bug defends itself in a big way! When threatened, the bombardier (bohm-BUH-duhr) aims the tip of its abdomen at its enemy and fires a spray of boiling chemicals.

WHERE TO FIND:
Bombardier beetles live on the ground in dirt or sandy areas. They inhabit many places around the globe.

NORTH AMERICA EUROPE
ASIA
SOUTH AMERICA AFRICA
AUSTRALIA

WHAT TO LOOK FOR:

✳ **SIZE**
They are ¼ to ⅝ of an inch long.

✳ **COLOR**
Their front wings can be black, orange, yellow, red, or metallic blue. They often have a yellowish brown head and legs.

✳ **BEHAVIOR**
The larvae eat the pupae, or young, of other insects.

✳ **MORE**
Bombardiers are not burned by the blast of chemicals they produce.

Like all beetles, the bombardier has hard front wings over a more delicate pair of wings it uses to fly.

GIANT WETA

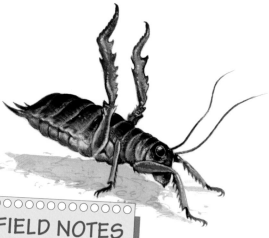

Found only in New Zealand, this huge, wingless insect looks like an overgrown cricket. It comes out at night to feed on plants and berries and hunt for small bugs.

FIELD NOTES

When faced by a hungry bird or lizard, the giant weta raises its spiny hind legs and kicks hard.

The giant weta (WEE-tuh) does not hop like crickets and grasshoppers. It walks from place to place.

NEW ZEALAND

Giant wetas once inhabited much of New Zealand but now survive only in nature preserves.

WHAT TO LOOK FOR:

✴ SIZE
This insect's body is four inches long. Its antennae can be the same length.

✴ COLOR
It is yellowish brown.

✴ BEHAVIOR
By day the giant weta hides in hollow trees and in bushes.

✴ MORE
The giant weta is also known by the names wetapunga and demon grasshopper.

SPINY KATYDID

Looking like a creature from another world, the spiny katydid is covered with thorns. Its prickly armor gives the bug some protection from the monkeys, birds, snakes, and spiders that like to eat it.

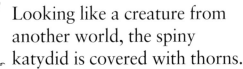

WHERE TO FIND:

SOUTH AMERICA

Spiny katydids make their homes in rain forests from Panama to southern Brazil.

WHAT TO LOOK FOR:

✴ SIZE
They are two to four inches long.

✴ COLOR
Spiny katydids are a leafy green color with yellow markings.

✴ BEHAVIOR
These thorny insects come down from trees at night to look for food on the ground. They eat fruits, plants, and caterpillars.

✴ MORE
Spiny katydids make a chirping sound.

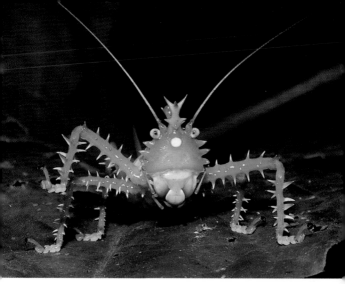

Thorns sharp as those of a rosebush cover all six of the spiny katydid's legs, as well as the sides and top of its head.

To defend itself from a monkey or other predator, this bug rises up and bats its front legs at the enemy.

DESERT LOCUST

 Many insects fly together in groups called swarms. The biggest swarms are formed by desert locusts. A single locust swarm can fan out over hundreds of square miles and include some 50 billion bugs.

WHERE TO FIND:

The desert locust is a type of grasshopper that inhabits dry areas in Africa, the Middle East, and Asia.

WHAT TO LOOK FOR:

✳ SIZE
Desert locusts are about two inches in length.

✳ COLOR
They are yellow and black or orange and black.

✳ BEHAVIOR
In dry times, when food is scarce, these insects live alone.

✳ MORE
Desert locusts swarm in years when rain falls and food is plentiful.

A young locust, or nymph, gets around by hopping. When it is fully grown, it will have wings to fly.

PAINTED GRASSHOPPER

 The bright colors that make this grasshopper so handsome to humans send a different signal to its predators. They are a reminder that this bug tastes bad.

WHERE TO FIND:
Look for this grasshopper in the deserts of the southwestern United States and northern Mexico.

UNITED STATES

MEXICO

WHAT TO LOOK FOR:

✳ SIZE
The painted grasshopper is $^3/_4$ to $1^3/_8$ inches long.

✳ COLOR
It has a multicolored pattern of blue, red, and yellow.

✳ BEHAVIOR
The female lays her eggs in soft soil in summer or fall. The eggs rest over the winter, then hatch in late spring.

✳ MORE
This grasshopper feeds on plants.

The painted grasshopper, which has short wings, cannot fly. It hops from place to place.

GIANT STICK INSECT

 The giant stick insect is not only one of the world's longest insects but also a camouflage expert. Its color and shape make it hard to see among leaves and twigs.

WHERE TO FIND:
Giant stick insects live on eucalyptus trees and shrubs in Australia and New Guinea.

NEW GUINEA

AUSTRALIA

WHAT TO LOOK FOR:

* SIZE
These big bugs are about one foot long.

* COLOR
Females are light brown in color; males are darker brown.

* BEHAVIOR
The female hangs upside down to lay eggs, using her abdomen to flick them away from the tree where she is hanging. The eggs look like plant seeds.

* MORE
Giant stick insects feed on leaves.

🕳🕳🕳🕳🕳🕳🕳🕳🕳🕳🕳🕳

FIELD NOTES

Just like a twig or leaf blown by a breeze, a stick insect sometimes sways gently from side to side.

Males, like this one, have long, slender wings. Females have short wings and do not fly.

FLOWER MANTIS

The flower mantis is a master of disguise. Looking like a delicate blossom, it waits for an unsuspecting insect to come within reach, then swiftly seizes and devours it.

A smaller version of the adult, the flower mantis nymph has legs shaped like flower petals.

WHAT TO LOOK FOR:

✳ SIZE
They are one to five inches long.

✳ COLOR
They are pink, white, orange, or a mixture of green with other colors.

✳ BEHAVIOR
Like all mantises, flower mantises prey on just about any insect or spider that comes their way.

✳ MORE
The flower mantis's disguise helps protect it from predators.

FIELD NOTES
This mantis looks so much like a flower that insects seeking nectar sometimes land right on top of it.

MADAGASCAR HISSING COCKROACH

When this roach is touched or threatened, it hisses so loudly that it can be heard 12 feet away. The sound startles predators, giving the bug more time to scurry away.

FIELD NOTES

This cockroach produces its hissing sound by forcing air through breathing holes on its abdomen.

These big cockroaches are wingless and hard shelled. They can live as long as seven years.

WHERE TO FIND:

AFRICA

The Madagascar hissing cockroach lives in forests on the island of Madagascar, off the east coast of Africa.

WHAT TO LOOK FOR:

✳ SIZE
Madagascar hissing cockroaches can be 2 to 3½ inches long.

✳ COLOR
They are leathery brown and black.

✳ BEHAVIOR
Males also hiss when they fight other males and when they are mating.

✳ MORE
Madagascar hissing cockroaches eat fruits that have fallen from trees.

PEANUT BUG

 This bizarre bug with a peanut-shaped head is also called the alligator bug. The front of its head looks like that of an alligator, complete with fake teeth and eyes. The resemblance may fool predators.

WHERE TO FIND:

The peanut bug makes its home in the rain forests of Central and South America.

SOUTH AMERICA

WHAT TO LOOK FOR:

＊SIZE
A peanut bug is three inches long.

＊COLOR
It is greenish brown with black, white, and reddish markings.

＊BEHAVIOR
To feed, the peanut bug pokes its straw-like mouth into a tree and sucks up sap.

＊MORE
Peanut bugs are hard to see from a distance because they blend in with the trunks of the trees that are their homes.

This bug has fake eyes near the top of its head. Its real eyes lie at the base of its huge head.

PERIODICAL CICADA

Among the loudest bugs in the world, male cicadas make a whirring sound to attract females. These insects appear in an area at periodic, or regular, intervals.

Periodical cicadas appear whitish for a while after molting, but their bodies soon harden and turn black.

WHERE TO FIND:
Periodical cicadas are found in wooded places in the eastern, southern, and midwestern United States.

WHAT TO LOOK FOR:

✳ SIZE
They are one to two inches long.

✳ COLOR
They have black bodies. Their eyes and wing veins are red.

✳ BEHAVIOR
A periodical cicada nymph lives underground for 13 or 17 years. It feeds on root juices during that time.

✳ MORE
In the spring of its 13th or 17th year, the cicada nymph emerges at night.

FIELD NOTES

After a cicada nymph leaves its burrow, it climbs a tree and molts, or sheds its skin. It is now an adult.

ASSASSIN BUG

 Assassin bugs come in many shapes and sizes, but they all kill the same way. They grab an insect with their front legs, stab it with their beak, and inject a poison. Then they suck out the victim's body juices.

WHERE TO FIND:
Over 5,000 kinds of assassin bugs live around the world in a variety of different habitats.

NORTH AMERICA EUROPE ASIA SOUTH AMERICA AFRICA AUSTRALIA

WHAT TO LOOK FOR:

✳ SIZE
Assassin bugs range from $1/3$ to $1^1/_2$ inches in length.

✳ COLOR
They come in many colors, including brown, black, and red. Some are colored to blend in with flowers.

✳ BEHAVIOR
Some assassin bugs guard their eggs from predators, such as wasps.

✳ MORE
Praying mantises eat assassin bugs.

Some assassin bugs, like this young bug spearing a fly, are long and slender. Others are oval shaped.

SHIELD STINKBUG

The shield stinkbug deserves its name for two reasons. First of all, its shape resembles that of a shield. Second, this little bug really can make a stink. It produces a smelly liquid that helps keep predators away.

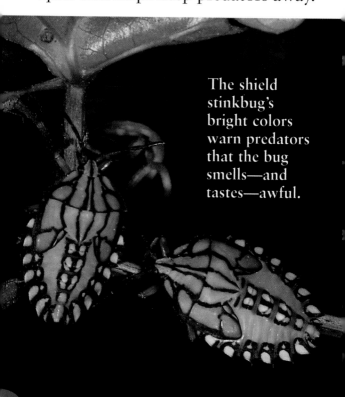

The shield stinkbug's bright colors warn predators that the bug smells—and tastes—awful.

WHERE TO FIND:
Thousands of kinds of shield stinkbugs inhabit the world. The most colorful ones live in tropical regions.

WHAT TO LOOK FOR:

✳ SIZE
They are ¼ to 1½ inches long.

✳ COLOR
They are green, brown, black, yellow, red, and blue. They can be one color or patterned.

✳ BEHAVIOR
Females lay their eggs in neat patterns on leaves.

✳ MORE
Most stinkbugs feed on plant juices, but some kinds prey on other insects.

BACKSWIMMER

Although it flies very well, the backswimmer spends most of its life floating upside down in the water. Insects that land on the water's surface risk being speared on its beak.

Accompanied by its reflection, a backswimmer moves through the water using its large hind legs as paddles.

WHERE TO FIND:
Backswimmers can be found in freshwater ponds and slow-moving streams in much of the world.

WHAT TO LOOK FOR:

✳ SIZE
They are about ¹/₂ of an inch long.

✳ COLOR
These bugs are cream colored or brown with dark legs and black eyes.

✳ BEHAVIOR
Backswimmers dive down deep at the first hint of danger.

✳ MORE
They store the air they need to breathe under their wings. When they run out of air, they return to the surface to get more.

HORNED TREEHOPPER

 Topped by a spiky hump, the horned treehopper does a great imitation of a plant thorn. Its spiny shape may make the bug painful for a bird or other predator to swallow.

WHERE TO FIND:
NORTH AMERICA

SOUTH AMERICA

The horned treehopper makes its home in warm, humid regions of North and South America.

WHAT TO LOOK FOR:

✳ **SIZE**
Most treehoppers measure $1/4$ to $5/8$ of an inch long.

✳ **COLOR**
Horned treehoppers are greenish in color with yellow or red markings.

✳ **BEHAVIOR**
Female treehoppers defend their young by buzzing and flapping their wings.

✳ **MORE**
Treehoppers are named for their jumping ability.

The horned treehopper has long legs for climbing and mouthparts for sucking plant juices.

43

DRAGONFLY

Dragonflies have been zooming around for more than 300 million years. These fast fliers were among the first insects on Earth. Some ancient dragonflies had wingspans of up to 30 inches.

WHERE TO FIND:
There are more than 5,000 kinds of dragonflies living in ponds and streams around the world.

WHAT TO LOOK FOR:

✻ SIZE
Dragonflies are ³/₄ to 6 inches long and have wingspans of 1 to 7 inches.

✻ COLOR
They can be blue, green, yellow, red, or brown. They are often metallic colors.

✻ BEHAVIOR
Dragonfly nymphs live in water for three months to four years, preying on insects, tadpoles, and small fish.

✻ MORE
Adult dragonflies hunt other insects.

Four powerful wings help the dragonfly to fly forward and backward, as well as to hover in midair.

GRAY WITCH MOTH

The gray witch moth holds the title for the largest wingspan of any butterfly or moth. Like witches in folktales, this gigantic moth takes to the skies after dark.

FIELD NOTES

When disturbed, this moth flashes bright white eyespots on the dark underside of its wings.

The wavy design on this moth's wings helps it blend in with tree bark, making it hard to see.

WHERE TO FIND:

The gray witch moth dwells in the rain forests of Central and South America.

WHAT TO LOOK FOR:

✳ SIZE
The gray witch moth can have a wingspan of 12 inches.

✳ COLOR
It is patterned with gray, white, and brown.

✳ BEHAVIOR
By day, the gray witch moth rests flat and still against the trunks of trees.

✳ MORE
It feeds on nectar from flowers during the night.

DEATH'S-HEAD HAWK MOTH

 The skull-like marking behind its head makes this furry moth one of the spookiest looking bugs. Hundreds of years ago, people thought it was a sign of bad luck or even death.

WHERE TO FIND:
This moth can be found in northern Africa and the Middle East, as well as in Europe.

EUROPE
ASIA
AFRICA

WHAT TO LOOK FOR:

✳ **SIZE**
The death's-head hawk moth has a wingspan of four to five inches.

✳ **COLOR**
It is black with orange-yellow markings.

✳ **BEHAVIOR**
When disturbed, this moth makes a high-pitched squeaking sound.

✳ **MORE**
It often invades beehives, where it steals honey.

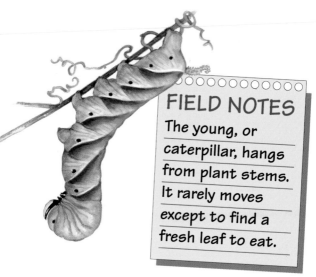

FIELD NOTES
The young, or caterpillar, hangs from plant stems. It rarely moves except to find a fresh leaf to eat.

The death's-head hawk moth has a sturdy body and streamlined wings. It is a very powerful flier.

MADAGASCAR SUNSET MOTH

In a bug beauty contest, the sunset moth of Madagascar would probably win first prize. Its brilliant colors shimmer with light, like the rainbow hues in a soap bubble.

Like a butterfly, this sunset moth perches with its wings folded up. Most moths perch with wings open flat.

WHERE TO FIND:
This lovely insect is found only on the island of Madagascar, off the east coast of Africa.

WHAT TO LOOK FOR:

✳ SIZE
The wingspan of the Madagascar sunset moth is about four inches.

✳ COLOR
It is velvety black with bright, shimmering bands of green, blue, orange, and purplish red.

✳ BEHAVIOR
Unlike most moths, which fly at night, this sunset moth is active during the day.

✳ MORE
As a caterpillar, it is yellow and black.

FIELD NOTES
In the late 1800s, women in Europe wore jewelry made from the colorful wings of this sunset moth.

51

AFRICAN BELLICOSE TERMITE

 These termites are master builders. They use soil mixed with their spit to build huge mound-like nests that dry hard as rock. One nest may hold up to five million termites.

WHERE TO FIND:
The African bellicose termite lives and builds its mounds in the grasslands of Africa.

AFRICA

WHAT TO LOOK FOR:

✱ SIZE
Most are less than an inch long.
A queen can be more than three inches.

✱ COLOR
Young termites are cream colored.
Adults are brownish.

✱ BEHAVIOR
A queen lays thousands of eggs a day.
The young are cared for by termites called workers.

✱ MORE
The termites eat wood and dried plants.

A winged adult termite, shown here with tiny workers and two young, will start a new colony.

FIELD NOTES
Bellicose termite nests can be 25 feet high. The height helps air flow, so the nest does not overheat.

TARANTULA HAWK WASP

The female tarantula hawk wasp can paralyze a tarantula with her sting! Then she drags it to her nest and lays an egg on it. When the egg hatches into a larva, it eats the spider.

FIELD NOTES

This fierce wasp hovers about its victim, then darts in to jab it near the head with its deadly stinger.

The male wasp, shown here, does not sting. Both male and female adult wasps feed on flower nectar.

The tarantula hawk wasp lives in desert areas of Mexico and the southwestern United States.

WHAT TO LOOK FOR:

* SIZE
The tarantula hawk wasp can be two inches in length.

* COLOR
It has a metallic bluish black body and orange wings.

* BEHAVIOR
A female lays 20 or more eggs and provides a tarantula for each one.

* MORE
This wasp's sting is very painful to humans.

VELVET ANT

 These insects look like cute furry ants, but it is best not to pick them up. Velvet ants are actually wasps, and the females deliver one of the most powerful and painful stings of any insect on Earth.

WHERE TO FIND:

NORTH AMERICA
SOUTH AMERICA
EUROPE
ASIA
AFRICA
AUSTRALIA

Velvet ants live in deserts, meadows, and forests throughout much of the world.

WHAT TO LOOK FOR:

✳ SIZE
Velvet ants are ½ to 1 inch long.

✳ COLOR
They can be black, red, or orange. Some have white or black markings.

✳ BEHAVIOR
Females invade the nests of bees or other wasps and lay their eggs on the larvae they find there.

✳ MORE
Velvet ants are also called cow killers because their sting is so strong.

FIELD NOTES

Female velvet ants have stingers but no wings. Males have wings but no stingers. They look less like ants.

The velvet ant's large antennae are very sensitive and help it find the nests of other wasps as well as those of bees.

ORCHID BEE

 Orchid bees are the prettiest bees as well as the fastest. Some tropical orchids can be pollinated only by male orchid bees, which are lured to the flower by its scent.

WHERE TO FIND:
Orchid bees make their home in the rain forests of Central and South America.

SOUTH AMERICA

WHAT TO LOOK FOR:

✳ **SIZE**
Orchid bees are ³/₈ to 1 inch long.

✳ **COLOR**
They come in several shiny, metallic colors, including green, blue, bronze, and purple.

✳ **BEHAVIOR**
The females of some orchid bees work together to build nests and raise their young.

✳ **MORE**
Their nests are often made with mud.

Orchid bees collect orchid fragrances on their body and store them in a spongy part of each of their hind legs.

○○○○○○○○○○○○

FIELD NOTES
The bucket orchid traps the orchid bee for 40 minutes so that it has plenty of time to pick up pollen.

LEAFCUTTER ANT

A leafcutter ant colony can have as many as five million members, each one with a job. Some cut leaves and carry them to the nest. Others use the leaves to grow a fuzzy fungus that feeds the whole colony.

WHERE TO FIND:
Leafcutter ants inhabit wooded land from the southern United States through South America.

WHAT TO LOOK FOR:

✱ SIZE
Leafcutter ants are $\frac{1}{16}$ to $\frac{1}{2}$ of an inch in length.

✱ COLOR
They are reddish brown.

✱ BEHAVIOR
The queen's only job is to lay eggs. She is the mother of every ant in the colony.

✱ MORE
A leafcutter nest may extend 25 feet below the ground and have hundreds of small rooms for growing fungus.

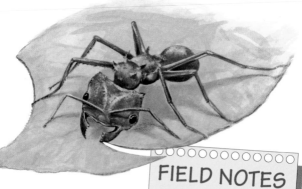

Smaller ants ride atop leaves toted by workers. Their job is to help defend the workers in case of attack.

GOLIATH BIRD-EATING SPIDER

This shaggy spider prowls South American jungles searching for insects, frogs, lizards—and baby birds—to eat. World's biggest spider, it is the size of a dinner plate.

SOUTH AMERICA

WHERE TO FIND:
The Goliath bird-eating spider dwells in the Amazon rain forest of South America.

WHAT TO LOOK FOR:

✳ SIZE
The Goliath bird-eating spider can be 3½ inches long, and its legs can span 11 inches. Its fangs are ½ of an inch long.

✳ COLOR
This huge spider is brown.

✳ BEHAVIOR
During the day, this spider hides on the ground in a burrow it lines with silk.

✳ MORE
Birds, reptiles, and frogs prey on young bird-eating spiders.

The hairs covering this spider's body and legs sense vibrations, which help alert it to prey or to predators.

The Goliath bird-eating spider injects venom into a bird or other prey, then sucks out its body juices.

SYDNEY FUNNEL WEB SPIDER

 Quick to attack, this Australian spider is one of the world's deadliest. A person bitten by it can become very sick and may even die if not treated with special medicine.

WHERE TO FIND:

AUSTRALIA

The Sydney funnel web spider lives only in southeastern Australia, around the city of Sydney.

WHAT TO LOOK FOR:

✳ SIZE
A female can be almost two inches long; males are about half that size.

✳ COLOR
This spider is black or dark brown.

✳ BEHAVIOR
The female spider rarely leaves its silk-lined, funnel-shaped underground web. The male roams in search of mates.

✳ MORE
This spider preys on insects that cross the lines of silk extending from its web.

FIELD NOTES

When disturbed, this spider lifts up its front legs and oozes a glob of poison from the tip of its fangs.

Found in forests and gardens alike, this funnel web spider has fangs so razor sharp that they can pierce a person's fingernail.

GOLDEN SILK SPIDER

 Webs woven by these spiders are so strong that they snare small birds. In tropical areas, the webs are so tough that even people can find it a challenge to get through one.

WHERE TO FIND:

Golden silk spiders dwell in woodlands and swamps in warm, humid parts of the world.

WHAT TO LOOK FOR:

✳ SIZE
Golden silk spiders can have bodies of one inch or longer.

✳ COLOR
They are golden or greenish brown with silvery white and black markings.

✳ BEHAVIOR
This spider paralyzes prey caught in its web with a quick bite, then wraps it in silk and saves it to eat later.

✳ MORE
Its webs can be more than six feet wide.

Native people in parts of Australia and New Guinea collect this spider's webs to make fishing nets.

This spider is named for the golden sheen of its large web.

67

TRAPDOOR SPIDER

The trapdoor spider specializes in surprise attacks. It lies hidden in its burrow until it feels the vibration of a passing bug. Then up it pops and seizes the startled prey.

Displaying the heavy body and thick, hairy legs typical of this bug, a trapdoor spider devours an insect.

NORTH AMERICA · EUROPE · ASIA · SOUTH AMERICA · AFRICA · AUSTRALIA

WHERE TO FIND:
Trapdoor spiders live in many parts of the world. They are most plentiful in warmer regions.

WHAT TO LOOK FOR:

✳ SIZE
Trapdoor spiders have a body length of one inch or more.

✳ COLOR
Most are brown or reddish brown.

✳ BEHAVIOR
They use the strong spines on their fangs to dig their burrows. Once the burrow is dug, they line it with silk.

✳ MORE
Trapdoor spiders usually guard their eggs until they hatch.

BOLAS SPIDER

The bolas (BO-luhs) spider is the only bug that lassos its meals. It spins a silky line with a gluey ball at the end. Then it swings the line toward moths that fly by. When the line strikes a moth, the spider hauls it in.

A bolas spider dangles its catch from a line. Like many spiders, it wraps its prey in silk.

WHERE TO FIND:
Bolas spiders can be found in wooded and shrubby places throughout much of the world.

WHAT TO LOOK FOR:

✳ SIZE
It is about ½ of an inch long.

✳ COLOR
Bolas spiders are light brown or green-ish and have fat, bumpy abdomens.

✳ BEHAVIOR
These spiders spend the day hiding among branches and leaves. They emerge at dusk and hunt all night.

✳ MORE
They are named after bolas, a kind of lasso used in South America.

FIELD NOTES
To lure male moths its way, the bolas spider releases a scent that mimics that of a female moth.

71

WATER SPIDER

 The water spider is the only spider that lives underwater. It spins a dome-shaped web in the water, anchors it to plants, and inflates the web with air it collects at the surface. This dome becomes the spider's home.

WHERE TO FIND:

EUROPE

ASIA

The water spider can be found in ponds and lakes in Europe and parts of Asia.

WHAT TO LOOK FOR:

✳ SIZE
The water spider is $\frac{1}{2}$ of an inch long.

✳ COLOR
It is dark brown or dark gray.

✳ BEHAVIOR
This spider rests in its dome with its legs sticking out. When it feels vibrations made by potential prey, it dives out to nab its dinner.

✳ MORE
The water spider mates and lays its eggs inside the dome it builds.

Away from its home, the spider gets the oxygen it needs from air bubbles trapped on its abdomen.

ANT-MIMICKING SPIDER

 Why would a spider imitate an ant? Mostly because ants taste bad, and that means predators pass them up. By looking like ants, these spiders avoid capture.

WHERE TO FIND:
There are many kinds of ant-mimicking spiders. The best mimics are found in warm regions of the world.

NORTH AMERICA
SOUTH AMERICA
AFRICA
ASIA
AUSTRALIA

WHAT TO LOOK FOR:

✳ SIZE
Most of these spiders are ¹/₄ to ³/₈ of an inch in length.

✳ COLOR
Their ant-shaped bodies can be black, brown, or orange.

✳ BEHAVIOR
Like ants, these impersonators run in a zigzag pattern.

✳ MORE
A few kinds of ant-mimicking spiders prey on the ants they imitate.

The ant-mimicking spider walks on six legs and waves its front two so they look like an insect's antennae.

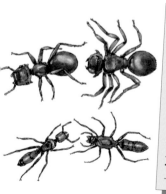

GLOSSARY

abdomen On an insect or spider, the rear segment of the body, which contains organs for digestion and reproduction.

antenna One of a pair of thin, segmented organs located on the head of an insect that help it smell, feel, and taste.

burrow A hole that an animal digs in the ground for its home.

caterpillar The worm-like larva, or young, of a moth or butterfly.

colony A group of insects that live together.

eyespots Bold, circular markings on an insect that resemble large eyes. They may help scare off enemies.

larva A stage in the life of many insects after hatching from an egg. A larva looks very different from an adult.

mate When an adult male and female come together to produce young.

nectar The sugary liquid made in a flower that attracts insects and other animals that spread the flower's pollen.

nymph A stage in the life of some insects after hatching from the egg. A nymph looks like an adult, but is smaller and lacks wings and the ability to mate.

pollen The fine powder made by flowers so they can reproduce. It is usually yellow.

pollination The process in which pollen is transferred from one flower to another of the same species to fertilize it—to make it produce seeds.

predator An animal that hunts and kills other animals for food.

prey An animal hunted for food.

pupa The resting stage of an insect as it transforms from larva to adult.

thorax The middle segment of an insect's body, to which its legs and wings are attached.

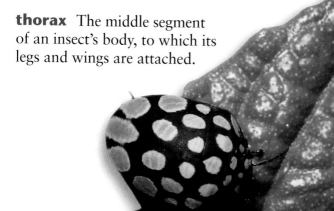

INDEX OF
WONDER BUGS

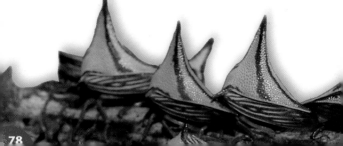

ABOUT THE CONSULTANTS

David W. Inouye is an ecologist and conservation biologist at the University of Maryland. He has studied insects and wildflowers at the Rocky Mountain Biological Laboratory since 1971. He researches ant-plant interactions and the bumble-bees, hummingbirds, and flies that pollinate wild-flowers that grow in the Colorado mountains.
Brian D. Inouye is an ecologist at the University of California. He has studied insects in the Rocky Mountains, California, and Central America. He currently researches parasitoids, which are insects that attack prey insects and lay eggs inside the victims. He also studies insects that cause plant galls.

PHOTOGRAPHIC CREDITS